Poems on Values to Succeed Worldwide in Life: Listening and Diversity and Unity

Simple and Insightful

O.K. FATAI

Pubished by OK Publishing

Wellington, New Zealand

Copyright © 2019 O.K. Fatai

Email: OK.Publishingnz@gmail.com

Full catalogue information may be obtained from the National Library of New Zealand

All rights reserved.

The moral right of the author has been asserted

ISBN-13: 978-0-9951213-3-1

All rights reserved. No part of this publication may be reproduced, stored in a retrieval system or transmitted in any form by any means electronic, mechanical, photocopying, recording or otherwise, without prior permission from the publisher.

DEDICATION

To all those who values the importance of having good listening skills and whose lives reflect good listening in their everyday interactions with others.

Contents

Feel important	10
Fully	11
That inner voice	12
Greatness	13
It shows	14
Value	15
Real simple	16
Really love	17
Inner	18
When we	19
There is	21
Should be	22
It's barbershop	23
We live	24
I hear	25
In the eyes	26
Driver	27
Love conquers all	28
So beneficial	29

Shining	30
Other books by O.K. Fatai	31
More books by O.K. Fatai	32
About the Author	34

ACKNOWLEDGMENTS

Family, friends and others, who had taught me the importance of having good listening skills.

Success Worldwide in Life through Listening

Feel important

When we listen
it makes the person talking

feel that he is respected
feel that he is important
feel that we care

about his ideas and voice
for this life is full of talkers
and doers

but less of people who are
willing to listen

and show that one really cares.

O.K. FATAI

Fully

There is silence
but there is no real listening

for real listening
is the full tuning of our hearts

to the heart and soul of
another person

for real listening
is done with the heart

mind and soul
and when there is real

listening, we will have
a society that is more

at peace with itself.

POEMS ON VALUES TO SUCCEED WORLDWIDE

That inner voice

We so much spend time
listening to the voices of others

and less and less time
listening to the inner voices
inside us

but it is equally important
to listen to what our hearts and souls

are saying to each of us
for listening to what is inside us

is the beginning of harmony and peace.

Greatness

There is energy in listening
there is force in listening

there is life in listening
there is greatness in listening

there is harmony in listening
there is peace in listening

so do listen to others
for it shows you are great

and someone with a lot of energy and life
yes, really great

with lots of energy and life.

It shows

The ability to listen
shows someone who cares

the ability to listen
shows someone who accepts

the ability to listen
show someone who is at peace

with oneself and others
for it is difficult to listen fully

when there is so much war inside
for it is difficult to listen

when the roars of hate is in our heart
so practice to love and accept yourself

so that you can become someone
exceptional in listening to other's voices.

O.K. FATAI

Value

People longed to know that their voices
are valued and their opinions matter

people longed to know that they are important
and that others view their voices

as something to take attention to
when we listen to what someone is saying

we are telling them that we value them
and we consider what they are saying as important.

Real simple

Listening is a simple thing to do
yet so many of us choose not to really listen

for even though we may be silent
we may not be really listening

for real listening is listening to what is said
and taking attention to what is not said

for it is by listening to the whole person
that we can really understand what someone

is really trying to tell us.

O.K. FATAI

Really love

When we really listen to what someone is saying
we are also saying to that person that we have real
love for that person

when we are really listening to the opinions of others
we are also telling that person that we have real
respect for them

when we are really listening to other's voices
we are really saying to that person that they
really matter to you.

POEMS ON VALUES TO SUCCEED WORLDWIDE

Inner

We listen to what others are saying
and we attempt to understand their message

but sometimes another important part
of listening is the ability to really listen

to the inner voice that we have
and really listen to what our soul is telling us

for it is important to listen to what the others
are saying, but it is equally important as well
to really listen to what our spirit is telling us.

O.K. FATAI

When we

When we really listen to what someone is saying
we are sending that person a message

that we have love in our hearts
when we really listen to what someone is telling us

we are sending a message to that person that
we have values and integrity in our souls

listening is not just being silent
it is also saying something about what we value

in our souls.

POEMS ON VALUES TO SUCCEED WORLDWIDE

Success Worldwide in Life through Diversity and Unity

O.K. FATAI

There is

Yes there is
in diversity
there is life

yes there is
in diversity
there are connections
yes there is
in diversity
there is love

yes there is
in diversity
there is richness

yes there is
in diversity
there are surprises

yes there is
in diversity
there is relatedness

yes there is
in diversity
there is complexity

yes there is
in diversity
there is you and me

all different
but all enriching.

Should be

Diversity should be encouraged
each of us has different talents

and many diverse talents
bringing unique abilities

all help to make a nation
have beauty and splendour

yes diversity so marvellous
and life enriching.

O.K. FATAI

It's barbershop

Their voices different
their melodies so inviting

and full of beauty to our hearts
all because they have diversity

of voices, but each brings together
harmony and magic.

POEMS ON VALUES TO SUCCEED WORLDWIDE

We live

We live with diversity of values
we live with diversity of cultures

we live with diversity of talents
we live with diversity of abilities

we live with diversity of backgrounds
all assisting in progressing humanity forward

and making this world a most interesting place.

O.K. FATAI

I hear

I hear the ostriches bleep
I hear the bats screech

I hear the bees hum and buzz
I hear the owls hoot and screech

I hear the bulls below
I hear the calves bleat

I hear the beetles drone
I hear the blackbirds whistle

I hear the bears growl
I hear the frogs croak and ribbit

I hear the giraffes bleat
I hear the hamsters squeak

I hear the pigs oint
I hear the pigeons coo

oh so much more interesting
to hear diversity of sounds!

In the eyes

In the eyes of me we have different cultures
in the eyes of me we have different backgrounds

in the eyes of me we have different talents
in the eyes of me we have different abilities

in the eyes of me we have different families
in the eyes of me we have different up bringing

in the eyes of me we have different thinking
in the eyes of me we have different strengths

however, in the eyes of my soul we are in unity
in the eyes of my soul we are common

in the eyes of my soul we are from the same place
in the eyes of my soul we have common ancestors

in the eyes of my soul we are one.

O.K. FATAI

Driver

Diversity is not a driverless car
driving aimlessly and not knowing

where it is heading
diversity is a car whose driver

is each of us all heading
towards a common goal

of unity and growing together
of a common goal of beauty

in diversity and golden in our unity.

Love conquers all

Love conquers all
for in our diversity

love brings us all together
to recognize that we are one

to celebrate our unity
even with all our differences

yes love is a magnet that draws
us together

love is a glue that bind our diversity together
and together we will remain strong.

O.K. FATAI

So beneficial

I consider it so beneficial
that we have diversity of thoughts

that we have diversity of ideas
that we have diversity of imaginations

for this world had made progress
in leaps and bounds

in all areas of civilization
all thanks to the diversities of our thoughts

and ideas and imaginations.

Shining

Diversity highlights differences
diversity promotes variety

in diversity we see beauty
in diversity we experience meaningfulness

and the more diversity we see
and experience in our journey

the greater the shining of the star
light that will guide us in both day and night.

Other books by O.K. Fatai

1. Poems on Values to Succeed Worldwide in Life: Being Responsible
2. Poems on Values to Succeed Worldwide in Life: Courage
3. Poems on Values to Succeed Worldwide in Life: Good Families
4. Poems on Values to Succeed Worldwide in Life: Forgiveness
5. Poems on Values to Succeed Worldwide in Life: Good Friends
6. Poems on Values to Succeed Worldwide in Life: Grace
7. Poems on Values to Succeed Worldwide in Life: Hope
8. Poems on Values to Succeed Worldwide in Life: Humility
9. Poems on Values to Succeed Worldwide in Life: Joy
10. Poems on Values to Succeed Worldwide in Life: Justice
11. Poems on Values to Succeed Worldwide in Life: Life
12. Poems on Values to Succeed Worldwide in Life: Love
13. Poems on Values to Succeed Worldwide in Life: Mercy
14. Poems on Values to Succeed Worldwide in Life: Peace
15. Poems on Values to Succeed Worldwide in Life: Perseverance
16. Poems on Values to Succeed Worldwide in Life: Faith
17. Poems on Values to Succeed Worldwide in Life: Harmony with Nature
18. Poems on Values to Succeed Worldwide in Life: Education

More books by O.K. Fatai

1. Poems on Values to Succeed Worldwide in Life: Understanding and Wisdom

2. Poems on Values to Succeed Worldwide in Life: Work and Optimism

3. Poems on Values to Succeed Worldwide in Life: Adversity and Confidence

4. Poems on Values to Succeed Worldwide in Life: Listening and Diversity and Unity

5. Poems on Values to Succeed Worldwide in Life: Sharing and Honesty

6. Poems on Values to Succeed Worldwide in Life: Simplicity and Harmony

7. Poems on Values to Succeed Worldwide in Life: Unity in Diversity and Connections

8. Poems on Values to Succeed Worldwide in Life: Contentment and Acceptance

9. Poems on Values to Succeed Worldwide in Life: Excellence and Compassion

10. Poems on Values to Succeed Worldwide in Life: Generosity and Being Passionate

11. Poems on Values to Succeed Worldwide in Life: Gentleness and Trustworthy

12. Poems on Values to Succeed Worldwide in Life: Patience and Being Tactful

13. Poems on Values to Succeed Worldwide in Life: Purity and Integrity

14. Poems on Values to Succeed Worldwide in Life: Being Modest

and Persistence

15. Poems on Values to Succeed Worldwide in Life: Respect and Loyalty

16. Poems on Values to Succeed Worldwide in Life: Self-Discipline and Orderliness

17. Poems on Values to Succeed Worldwide in Life: Service and Going the Extra Mile

18. Poems on Values to Succeed Worldwide in Life: Sincerity and Honour

19. Poems on Values to Succeed Worldwide in Life: Nature and Reliability

20. Poems on Values to Succeed Worldwide in Life: Helpfulness and Consideration

21. Poems on Values to Succeed Worldwide in Life: Preparedness and Visionary

22. Poems on Values to Succeed Worldwide in Life: Reverence and Thankfulness

23. Poems on Values to Succeed Worldwide in Life: Wonders and Cooperation

About the Author

O.K. Fatai is a poet and author from Wellington, New Zealand. He likes to spend time writing poems, especially ones that explore the different aspects of values and virtues that are widely accepted in different cultures today.

O.K. Fatai also likes to write songs and some of his forthcoming books are song lyrics that also look at different values and virtues and some of their appeal to us today. In his spare time, he writes short stories and novels. He is looking forward to sharing these stories with readers around the world, and he has already published some short stories and has more than ten forthcoming publications in children's literature. O.K. Fatai is also writing novels for young adults and adults. He is also a playwright and has written and/or directed more than eight short plays.

He likes painting abstract art and enjoys the different interpretations of abstract paintings, especially when they reflect values and virtues. He is also a photographer who likes to take photographs of nature and the environment, which has a special place in his heart. He is keen on filming and editing videos as well, plays musical instruments and is part of a local band.

O.K. Fatai is a volunteer at the United Nations and regional prisons in Wellington and, for many years, had volunteered to more than ten other organizations. He works in the health sector and is also a consultant for three different online companies, and the President and CEO of more than three businesses. He is also available as an external consultant to the United Nations, the European Bank for Reconstruction and Development, and the Asian Development Bank.

O.K. FATAI

POEMS ON VALUES TO SUCCEED WORLDWIDE

www.ingramcontent.com/pod-product-compliance
Lightning Source LLC
Chambersburg PA
CBHW020432010526
44118CB00010B/537